Copyright © 2018 by Aicha Ayana

All rights reserved. This book or any portion thereof may not be reproduced or used in any manner whatsoever without the express written permission of the author except for the use of brief quotations in a book review.

Printed in the United States of America

First Printing, 2018

ISBN-13: 978-1718699175

ISBN-10: 1718699174

www.womanupnetwork.org

The Diary of a **BROKEN** Woman

Instead of dedicating this book to someone I know, I've decided to dedicate it to you. The woman fighting to know and understand herself, her struggle, and her life. The woman trying to make sense of it all. The woman who is broken but trying to put herself back together. Remember your broken pieces STILL make a beautiful collage.

Often times we're told we're too confident, too proud…. Keep calm. But I don't want to keep calm. I want to live out loud. I want to live in color. – Aicha Ayana

I went through a bad breakup a while back that almost broke my soul. I tried my best to keep it together on the outside, while on the inside I was falling apart. It made me wonder how many other women are fighting the same battle. Smiling on the outside but struggling on the inside. I decided to write this so that others know they are not alone.

This book shares some of my deepest thoughts and experiences with hopes to set others on the journey to heal, evolve, and create a beautiful life **with** their scars. What you're freed from can no longer hurt you.

By God, I am free.

-Aicha

Feb. 28th, 2013

"I'm almost 30 years old and I've seemed to hit a dead end in life. I have no husband, no real career, no real friends, goals or even motivation. I think if it wasn't for my kids, I probably would be suicidal. I can't tell anyone how I feel out of embarrassment. Someone once told me the price of popularity was high. I never thought to the point it would equal depression.

I feel like I've thrown my whole life away. Everything good, I've let pass me. Now I'm stuck building things I should've so long ago. I can understand why some celebrities commit suicide.

They feel like they have no one to share their innermost feelings with or that truly loves them. You have to sort of keep this fake smile that everything is okay when in reality, everything is a disaster.

I watched a movie some months back. The girl was me. Silently crying for peace. She had everything but still was so alone."

2013 was my year of breakdown. I had lived so crazy in the previous years that it was all starting to weigh heavily on me. Facing reality is a harsh thing when you're not ready to see things for what they are. Somehow God made me. I was a walking disaster. A functioning loser. Someone who was essentially a waste of existence. That hurts my heart to even write that. Sometimes we look back on life thinking what really have we done, or accomplished.

One of my greatest accomplishments by far has been my children. I think their existence is what kept me strong during these years. I knew I had to be there for them. I knew I had to win for them. Not everyone has children though. In instances like that who do you stay strong for? It's easy. You stay strong for yourself.

Life was not meant to be easy. I strongly feel each of us was put here to go through some type of hardship. Those hardships are to either teach us faith, a lesson, or a testimony to save someone else. With me, it has been a mixture of both. I feel the bigger portion, however, was to impact the world. "Healers" experience so many different trials and tribulations. I cannot expect to change the world unless I myself have experienced hurt. It took me years to understand that concept.

I'm not sure where exactly you are in life right now. Maybe you're comfortable and happy (it's a good chance you aren't if you bought a self-help book though) but know that the journey is required to get you to the place of a breakthrough. The journey is necessary for growth. You may feel like you're on a dead-end road. Headed nowhere fast, but the power of persistence is REAL. Hang tight.

    Things may be stagnant for months. Maybe even years, then BOOM! Here comes the overflow. Here comes the increase. Here comes the abundance. The best advice I can ever dish out is to TRUST the process. You have to go through THAT to get to THIS. You cannot cheat the process. Life knows exactly what you've given. It's a time to reap and a time to sow. Trust that process.

March 11th, 2013

"Today we went to church. When it came to offering time, I looked in my purse and had two bills. $1.00 and $100.00. At first, I put the dollar in the envelope but thought how I was cheating God. I put the $100 in instead. I pray God sends me financial increase. Jadyn (my daughter) asked to be baptized today. I was so happy. The kids bring me so much peace. Everything I've searched for in the world is right in them.

Life is not perfect, but when I look back over these past years, I could've been killed, raped, in jail or anything else but God has kept me. I don't know why. I look at my sister sometimes with such envy. She has everything (education, career, family) and did it on her own. Everything was given to me and I still messed up. How??

It's a purpose for all though and all things a purpose. God wanted me with this testimony for a reason. To whom much is given, much is required. I was given many gifts. Maybe it's because I'm not using them God decided to take them away. I don't know about anything anymore. I just need direction and guidance. What is it that I'm doing wrong? What is it that I need to do right? Please, God, send me some kind of sign."

When I read this entry in my diary the first thing I thought of was why I was too blind at that time to see the things I did have. Sometimes we're too blind to see that the best blessings are right in front of our face. During this time, I was too focused on the things I did not have. Even though it was small, I had money in my pocket, a child that was trying to be obedient in Christ, and livelihood. That didn't impress me obviously. I wanted a big house, nice car, six-figure job, and a fat bank account. Not even realizing people with all of those things can still be miserable.

Over time, I have learned that God will not send you more blessings until you're thankful for the ones you have. Being ungrateful takes away so many things that were intended for us. If we keep our eyes on our own lives instead of other's we can realize we're more blessed than we think.

We go on this quest for life thinking if we just have more of what someone else has, we will be happy. Happiness is not brought through items, material things or anything else that can be purchased. It may give you temporary satisfaction but for long-term, the feeling will slowly go away. Happiness is truly brought to us by the things that cannot be purchased.

Look around. Take time to analyze your life. What is it that you DO have? What is it that makes you happy? What is it that if it was taken away from you right at this instant would hurt you? Value those things. Treasure those things. Lift those things up high.

Simple things such as health, food, and even waking up in the morning are things we take for granted. A heartbeat in your chest is doing better than the person who did not wake up this morning. How often do we sit, and just think about that? I know I don't quite often. Figure out what in life is your reason for living and sculpt your life around that. There is an old saying that in order to receive abundance, you have to be grateful for the small things you have now.

     I have truly learned to be happy with whatever it is I have, knowing the power of being thankful will bring me so much more. Grateful is a state of mind that radiates on such a high frequency that it allows room for so many other blessings. Make that choice over your life. Look at the glass half full, instead of half empty. No matter how bad things are, they can always be worse. Live life with no regrets HAPPY for whatever it is you have been blessed with.

June 1st, 2013

"I had the worst encounter ever with a guy I met. Us "talking" has only lasted two good months and ended up with me finding out he had a girlfriend. I was so embarrassed. I was essentially bragging about him in the salon, and out pops this girl who says "That's ***** boyfriend." I felt like a real dummy.

When I confronted him about the situation, he claimed they are no longer together. I don't know what to believe. I mean early morning AND late-night texts, calls, facetimes. How does he even function in a relationship? Maybe he is telling the truth. WHO KNOWS! Lord, I can never figure out why men LIE."

I was still hurting from my previous relationship when I met Troy. I'm unsure if that clouded my judgment or what but baby I was head over heels instantly. Our days were spent texting each other, our nights were spent together out on the town. I had been told he had a girlfriend, but when I confronted him about it, he said their relationship was over. I believed him.

One night we took a "selfie" which I posted to my social media page. Just as I had been afraid of, someone must've gotten in contact with ***** because she wrote me asking who I was, and what did him and I have going on. I didn't respond. He called me soon after laughing about the post. I didn't realize it then, but any man that finds two women arguing over him funny isn't a man at all. I felt guilty and beyond humiliated. Troy not only played games with me, but he played with a woman he had been with for years.

One thing I have learned over the years is that NO REAL MAN WILL EVER PUT YOU INTO A SITUATION WHERE YOU'RE QUESTIONING YOUR WORTH, TITLE, OR SELF RESPECT.

So often we look at the other woman as the cause or root of a man's infidelities. It is not the other woman's fault because most of the time, they are being told lies such as I was. A big problem is that we don't hold our men accountable for their actions! We forgive time after time and welcome the dogs back with open arms! It goes beyond cheating too. Diseases are REAL and most of the strays aren't protecting themselves.

The other point of view lies with the "side chick", the role I played. While some of us get the wool pulled over our eyes by these men lying, there is still a huge amount of us who just don't care if a man has a girlfriend or not. I remember in the beauty shop hearing so many women saying after they've been glammed up how they were "going to find somebody's man to take tonight". Is that what we've come to as sisters? Taking pride in seeing the next woman hurt? How can that even be our intentions want to see the next woman's relationship fail?

In relationships, one thing all of us will learn is that if he cheats on her, he will cheat on you. There is no different magic trick you can do to keep him. If he's not happy in his relationship, he has the option to leave. Do not be fooled into the foolery they try to make you believe that they are staying because of some other reason other than they simply WANT to be there. They want her, you, she, and them. Cake and ice cream with a soda on the side. What you allow will continue.

Every time I see the meme "God did not create you to be a side chick" I laugh. It's the absolute truth! Not only did he not create any of us to be side chicks, he did not create any of us to be used, abused and or cheated on. Troy and I stopped talking that day. Not because he decided to not continue a fling with me, but because I chose my self-respect over his shenanigans. If you're ever faced with this scenario, I would hope you don't allow the wool to be pulled over your eyes, but that you clearly understand your worth to realize you deserve more.

August 18th, 2013

"Damien called me today to wish me a happy belated birthday. I haven't talked to him in years. What a joke. He must not remember how many bruises I've had courtesy of him. We were together for two years. Now that I really look back on it, I don't know how in the world I ever got through two years of that. Living in fear.

It's scary because you don't know what's next, you just hope for the best. I never saw anything like that growing up. Lord knows I tried to shelter my kids away from it as much as possible."

When I met Damien, he was sweet as pie. He was the perfect guy to my children and me. We had nothing in common except the attraction we had for each other. I thought that would be enough. As time went by, things became different. Damien got more and more aggressive with me. It started with his words, then went to threats, and finally progressed to the first time he hit me. I remember it vividly.

I had just gotten my wisdom teeth pulled a few days before. We went to a gas station for ice. While Damien waited in the car, I went inside. There was a guy who offered to get the ice out of the cooler for me. I guess he had been watching from outside the guy and I talking because when I came back to the car an instant argument started.

He accused me of flirting with the guy. Before we could even get out of the gas station parking lot, he punched me in my face. Blood flew everywhere. That was the first time. It wasn't the last.

The behavior continued. Whenever he got upset, I took cover. Sometimes I couldn't get away and would have to fight him back best I could. I remember looking at women on Lifetime always thinking I could never be them. There was no way I could EVER let a man beat me. I had spoken too soon because here I was taking punch after punch.

It's hard to judge women who stay in these situations. For me, it was out of pity. I think a little for him and a little for me. Damien had no family. Neither did I. I thought that if I left him (or kicked him out because after all, he was staying in MY house), that I would have failed him. I took that same scenario to heart for myself as well. That if I indeed did break up with him, I would have no one. As long as we were together we had each other. That made it okay, right?

Things got worse and worse. One day so bad the neighbors called the cops. When they got to the house, I had bruises from a previous occasion. He was instantly put in handcuffs. When the cops got called to the house, they had alerted DCF. DCF had required me to attend mandatory counseling. During one of my counseling sessions, I remember being told, "Abusers don't stop abusing. They don't know how to stop". It was like a light clicked on.

What she had told me was the truth. **Abusers do not stop abusing. It's not going to get better. They are not going to just wake up one day and stop. Things are not going to change.** We misinterpret so many of our feelings into thinking situations such as these are love. Please let me stress this if you have never heard it before, **LOVE DOES NOT HURT OR DRIVE YOU CRAZY.** The right man will never hurt or harm you in any way, shape, or form. They will build you up and never break you down.

We become so convinced that if we just stick around long enough, they will change. They won't. Having kids really complicates the situation because even if they don't see you getting hit, they see your bruises or feel your mood. My kids are notorious for feeling my moods. They can tell when I'm sad without me even speaking a word. How unfair is that to a child to have a parent who is fighting situations such as these in their own home?

The words that counselor told me that day, changed my life. I have applied them to so many different scenarios. Abusers don't stop abusing.

Liars don't stop lying. Cheaters don't stop cheating. I can go on and on. You will basically be at a crossroads of choosing them or choosing you. Despite how much I thought I loved Damien, I made one of the best decisions of my life. To never accept him back. I chose me. I loved him, but I loved me more and I loved my kids even more than that.

September 17th, 2013

"As much as I try to forget about it I can't. The 5th year anniversary of when I committed murder. I killed my own flesh and blood. A creation of me. Whenever I think of my abortion, I cry. Hopefully, God and my child can forgive me. I was scared. Scared of doing it alone again. I wonder does the baby still exist. Does it hate me? Can I see them one day to apologize?

I conceived a child with a man I knew I had no future with. For that, I don't think I can ever forgive myself. It was still mine though. Does that make me less of a mother? When I look back on my life and all the mistakes I made, it sickens me to my core. I messed up so bad."

At the time I got pregnant, I already had my three children. I felt complete and my plate was more than full. You might be wondering why I was even doing certain activities to get pregnant if I knew I couldn't take care of another child. Unfortunately, birth control doesn't always work. When I first found out, initially I prayed for strength to take care of another child. I swear I thought I was superman, and if I could do it with the three kids I already had, taking on a fourth wouldn't be so hard.

Over the next few weeks, I told a few people about my pregnancy. Everyone told me how I could not possibly take care of another child. I heard so much negativity that it took me to the place where I thought I could not take on another child financially or even mentally. I made the decision to abort.

I remember being embarrassed even walking into the abortion clinic. I knew I was doing something wrong. My hands shook as I filled out papers and my heart was beating so fast as if I could feel each pump. I got a white cover and was told to undress from the waist down. Tears flowed. I don't want to go too much in depth about the procedure because I don't think I'm ready to share those feelings with the world.

Afterward, the nurse took my blood pressure. She said my heart was beating so fast I could potentially have a heart attack. They gave me some kind of medicine to calm me down. As I looked around the recovery room with other women who had aborted, everyone seemed perfectly fine. Watching TV, texting, and even smiling. Was this normal? Was everyone supposed to be okay after something so traumatizing?

As I write this chapter, I've had to pause and take breaks multiple times. It's a different kind of hurt I'm still not equipped to deal with.

I spoke to a friend of mine, Tony, a few days after. I asked him on judgment day would I be judged for my decision. God would ask me "why" and I would say, "I wasn't strong enough", and he would reply, "I always got you through everything else, why couldn't you trust me this time too?". As much as felt like I wasn't ready to share this personal story of mine, I felt the need to. I felt that it was important for the world to know there is a higher being out there that will provide strength, purpose, and guidance if you TRUST.

Do not let the words of others force you to do something that you really don't want to do or to keep you from doing something you really want to do. The funny thing about life is it has no do-overs. We only get ONE shot. Don't make a decision based on someone else's opinion when it's a chance you'll regret it later on. Do what's best for YOU. Not what anyone else THINKS is best. To this day, I think about my baby. I had planned to name it Chazz. I had a baby book made and all. I look at it around the same time each year.

Whenever I think of the memory of the child I did not have, my soul aches. To this day I battle with feelings of loss, regret, and sorrow. I made a choice that I have to live with for the rest of my life. My individual situation applied to my pregnancy, but your individual story may be something different.

If you're ever faced with making a choice that could potentially change your life, please make sure you're making whatever choice for YOU not because of what someone else told you to do or not to do. Live life with no regrets no matter what the situation is. The only thing guaranteed to you in life is you. Make sure she's set up to win at all times.

October 1st, 2013

"I've been thinking about starting some type of girl power group. Hopefully, connect with other women, offer some inspiration, heal each other. Today, I cried a few times. Each time, I caught myself and started praising the Lord for the good. It made me smile. God is real.

This whole transition thing is going to be a journey, but I sincerely believe God has me 1000. All things through and by faith. Reading the bible yesterday, I stumbled across this verse, "For I know the plans I have for you, plans to give you hope and a future." I'm holding onto that promise. These next few weeks, I know he's about to show out for me! God is coming through with victory!"

The power of the mind is real. When I stumbled across this entry I smiled. Thoughts of WomanUp even back then. What more so caught my attention was how I continued to trust in the promise better is guaranteed to all of us. No matter what your religious beliefs are one thing is clear, we all have the tools we need to create a beautiful life. If you've heard me publicly speak, you know that is one of my favorite sayings. I use it on my print materials, t-shirts, and even when I sign books. I firmly believe in that promise.

My mother was a hard-working woman. She had 4 of us and always seemed to have my Aunt's kids too. She was a great mother, I can NEVER take that away from her, but her time was limited being she always was at work. I didn't have too many "role-models" growing up. My sister was an overachiever but being we were so far apart in age, we really didn't bond in ways most sisters do. I was left with figuring out life on my own. I didn't know what my strengths were or even weaknesses (I'm actually still finding out to this day). I sort of went with the flow my whole life. It wasn't until my late 20's that I decided to seek purpose and not until my 30's I began to understand just who Aicha was.

For so many years, I thought I lacked certain things to have a good life. I didn't. What I lacked was vision. We have been equipped with so many different qualities that we don't even understand how powerful we really are. I firmly believe that when God put us here, he gave each and every one of us something different. You may be good in public speaking, she may be great at drawing. He may be a great runner, but his brother may be a phenomenal swimmer. It's up to each of us to find what works for us and use it to its full potential.

We can ultimately create whatever life we want for ourselves based on our strengths alone. Explore your strengths, but also embrace your weaknesses. Failure, after all, will teach you lessons nothing or no one else can. Take your lesson, move from it and grow from it. Don't spend much time revisiting why something didn't work. So many of us choose to stay looking at a closed door that we don't even realize there is one right around the corner that is open for us. I said in a previous chapter to trust your process. I'm going to go a step further with this part and say to not only trust your process but to trust yourself.

It's okay if you don't know your strengths. The advice I give to people to help figure them out is to keep a journal. Your most private intimate thoughts are voiced there. It gives you an outlet like no other source. Write in it every day, but also have times where you just go back and read. You'll learn more about yourself than you ever knew. Trust me. You are reading mine, right? Trust the strengths God gave you, and trust that they will work for you, and forever to your advantage. You lack NOTHING in life. Use the gifts you were given.

Nov. 4th, 2013

"This year has truly flown by! I've been going back and forth with USF about attending graduate school. It's so high, and I don't have that type of money right now. I have to save every last penny, especially since I'm not working.

I hosted a hair show in Gainesville this past weekend. I swear no matter what I do, whenever I touch the mic it feels so real. I know one day I'm going to be some sort of professional host or speaker. I talked to Nola about it today. He said that what I post on social media inspires people including him and that it's time to open up to people.

I had planned on doing this, but I'm scared of being judged. I do want to do some sort of empowerment event soon. Lack of funds is keeping me from it right now though. I'll just keep praying and I know God will find a way."

(I'm spending multiple chapters talking essentially about purpose because the need for all of us to find ours is so important).

I never write anything before I go into an event (unless it's a class or seminar where I have to teach something). I think it's fake. What's truly in your heart should flow out. This may be the reason I usually end up crying at events and holding up everyone's program. I want people to have the authentic Aicha though.

I was at an event for teen moms a few months back that a friend asked me to come speak at. I got this feeling to start talking about purpose. What came out next moved the whole room including the adults there. "Never chase the money, chase your passion. The money will come on its own as long as you follow your purpose". I didn't know the effect it really had on everyone including myself until I replayed a video someone had of me recorded from the event saying it. I think we all get wrapped up in the hype of wanting to make money that we forget about doing the things we love. We forget about what it is that makes us happy.

If you would've told me years ago I would've been a public speaker, I would have laughed. There would've been no way I would've ever seen myself standing in front of hundreds of people telling not only my story but encouraging women everywhere to "WomanUp". God had other plans though.

My mom said she always thought I was going to be a pastor growing up. She said I would walk around the house with the Bible in my hand preaching Bible stories, and how everyone needed to do right in life. When I look back on it now, it was if God was getting me prepared as a little girl to do exactly what it is I do now. Maybe not preach the gospel but speak comfortably to people about the path to success.

No matter what I've ever done in life, there has been no feeling to compare to the tingling I get when I touch the microphone. There is no feeling compared to when I look in the eyes of women who shared the same struggles as I. There is no feeling compared to when someone emails me or direct messages me that something I said or did changed their life. No feeling at all.

We each have a calling inside of us to do something great. Something to change the world. Something that when you do it, it gives you gratification unlike you ever felt. If you're unsure what yours is, do this brief task. Get a piece of paper. Write at the top "what is my purpose". Write down any and everything you can think of that moves you, inspires you, or motivates you. When you reach the one that makes you cry, that is your purpose. That is what you've been put here to do, accomplish, and change the world with. Find what it is and go do it. Then go change the world.

Dec. 1st, 2013

"Today church was amazing. I felt the whole service. We go through so much, but it's nothing God can't solve. You have to give your problems to him and thank him in advance for bringing you out.

The pastor said it's a young lady in an abusive relationship that God is getting ready to bring you out of. I believe that woman is me. Even though Marion has never hit me, the abuse is mental, and I think sometimes mental abuse can be way worse than physical. That man has brought me to an all-time low and it seems like he leaves me there. The worst feeling in the world is to open up to someone and they use it against you. I've been praying so hard lately for favor. Today, I made the proclamation that **_it is done_**."

At first, the parties were cool. It was fun. I loved that we got so much attention, and everybody respected us. Then I started to hate it. I wanted to be normal. I wanted to live normal. House with a picket fence, and a few dogs normal. Mario didn't. There is a saying I've seen on social media before, "Some people hustle to be seen, others hustle to not be seen". Marion was one who wanted to be seen.

When we first started dating, I accepted this behavior. I wanted to be seen too. It was seemingly a goal for me to be the limelight of wherever I went. I was. I can't say what exactly shifted in me to want better for myself than just a champagne bottle, and a couch to stand on in the nightclub. I like to think it was simply God moving in my life. When I did decide there were things I wanted to do for self-improvement such as going back to school, opening a store, and starting this very journey I'm on now, it was if he got upset. I talk about this behavior in my book, "I had to WomanUp", but I'm going to write extensively about those feelings now.

Mario was upset not only that I wanted to "level up", but that I wanted him to as well. These are the type of relationships that you have to be extremely cautious of. A big factor in life is to always want more. More for you, more for your family, more for your children. So many people are stuck and happy with being complacent. Complacency is the worst place you could ever be in. He was happy with having the money to do fun things, but I was no longer satisfied with fun things. I didn't want to be able to buy a section at a nightclub anymore, I wanted to be able to own the building.

Before I bring new people in my life, I ask them what they are doing in their own life. What their dreams are, hopes, and aspirations. You can tell a lot about a person simply by asking them those things. If they have none or don't have any that quite make sense, do yourself a favor and run. Escape a situation that can potentially drain you. Even if you decide to stick around, you'll end up being forced away anyway.

People who don't have the same will or drive as you have a way of making others that do feel uncomfortable. I can notice it now for myself a mile away. When I walk into the wrong room, others will judge me instantly off of my good energy. If it's other people in the room with like energy as I, they will gravitate, but if its negative energy, often negative conversations, feelings, and thoughts from those people occur. People will rip you to shreds simply because you vibrate high.

When I was dating Mario, I didn't understand this. I thought that maybe I was doing something wrong or that I was a bad person. It wasn't that at all. It was that my dreams were too big for him. If your dreams and goals are too big for the people around you, then its time to find some new people to surround yourself with whether that be family, friends, or a significant other.

It's okay to outgrow people. In order to get to a new level, we must shed certain things around us. Most of the time those "things" happen to be people. Do whatever you can to protect your peace, goals, and dreams. Science tells us that energy can't be created or destroyed, it can only be transferred. Isn't that enough proof why it's so important to surround ourselves with positive beings?

Jan. 27th, 2014

"I woke up this morning crying, and still do not have a reason why. I felt so alone. Depressed. Evolution is a good thing, but often times very depressing. Trying to figure out what I need to do in life, who I need to leave behind, and where I'm going is so confusing. Lord guide me.

I got a job last week. Mainly because I still had no stable income. I didn't last one week. I quit. The boss I guess came out of me. Maybe I should say pride. I just felt like it wasn't for me. Why work for someone else when I can work for myself? I want my own business, but what do I do? I want to sell clothes again, but everyone sells clothes now. Ughhhh! What to do? I just hope I can keep everything together for the kid's sake.

I cried so long today that I couldn't even look at myself in the mirror, and when I finally did, there was an expression I will never forget. Pure pain. Pain from what though? Problems I caused on myself? I feel like such a fucking loser.

I planned on shutting down my social media for a few months just to try and find me. I need a break from the world, and the drama on these sites seem to consume me. I only want to be surrounded by positive people and things. I've allowed so many negative things cause me to be negative. I want to release and move on. I just want to enjoy life to the fullest.

I have an appointment to see a therapist tomorrow. I know I need help dealing with the wounds of my past. I just want to heal and grow."

Each of us has been here. WTF am I doing in life? I've tried, and nothing works. Now I'm back to square one. Please let me stress this if no one else ever has, **falling down is not defeat**. Looking back during this time, I thought I should've been in a different place in my life. I was too old to be trying to piece things together. What's too old though?

We've let society put timelines on when we should do things and have certain things accomplished not realizing life has its own plans. For the life of me, I couldn't figure out why things wouldn't work in the ways I needed them to. It was because I was trying to follow "traditional" beliefs instead of venturing out on my own path. So many things influence us to believe we're not doing enough. You can never do enough though for a destiny that wasn't meant for you.

You will always fail trying to force something that was never meant to be.

How many of us actually live our OWN lives? Not the live our parents wanted for us, or our spouse, but that life we want for ourselves? I didn't realize these things about myself until I decided to seek help from a therapist. Therapy helped me to see my life for what it really was. Life sometimes weighs us all down in ways that we have to piece ourselves back together. The wounds of our broken-ness run too deep.

Some of my insecurities about me not being in the place I wanted to be in life amounted to me not being able to see my life for what it really was. Instead, I was envisioning myself as a loser when in reality, I was creating my own lane. My own life and on my terms. That's something we all have to embark on by ourselves. EACH JOURNEY

WILL BE DIFFERENT BECAUSE EACH LIFE IS DIFFERENT. You cannot calculate where you need to be based on where someone else is or what new statistic comes out.

If you have experienced these same feelings, please know that you ARE NOT A LOSER. You're indeed a winner. You can do, be, and accomplish anything you want in life on your own timeline. Yes, its cool to get it right the first time, but even if you don't, think of it as you are warming up for the second go around. Accept nothing but positive thoughts about yourself. Anything negative is rejected.

April 22nd, 2014

"I'm going to start the women's group. I don't even know if it's going to be approved by others. Won't know until I try, I guess. I want to write a book too. Would anyone even be interested in my life? My biggest enemy has been myself all of these years. I doubt me. I set myself up to fail before anyone else does.

I made a post on IG today about love and how a man will make you feel so low and unloved. It got all type of comments and likes. It hurt my heart to know so many other women hearts ached as mine does. That's the basis of what I want to do. To let people know they are not alone."

"What will they think" has killed more dreams than anything in this world. Newsflash! FUCK WHAT THEY THINK. Please forgive me for my wording, but that's honestly how I feel. How many of us have dreams and things we really want to do, but we're worried about if it will be accepted or not?

When we first started in 2015, I remember I was nervous. Not only about losing money but about if people would accept the program. I remember talking to our President at the time saying, "what if it fails". I will never forget her response. She looked at me and said, "but what if it flies". What if….

Long story short, we ended up investing all of this money in our first program which was a flop. I think 30 people showed up. I was heartbroken. It was a blow to the gut because I'm thinking here I am trying to do something positive, that failed. Despite failure, we kept going.

Three years later, we have built a chain of Tampa's largest expos, seminars, classes, conferences, retreats, brunches, and networking events. I've lost track of how many members WomanUp has and events we've held between the WomanUp expo, the WomanUp foundation, and the WomanUp Network. I know it's a lot though. God, it's a surreal feeling even thinking of it. I have helped create not only a brand but a platform and presence for myself that is undeniable. How did I do it? By not giving a damn what anyone had to say or think about what I was doing.

I was told along my journey that what I was doing would never prosper. I wasn't liked enough in the area to attract people out. It was impossible to change my old party girl image into something positive.

Man were they wrong. Initially it hurt to think people right around me couldn't see my vision (usually that's how it is), but after a while, I stopped letting anything that didn't motivate me to penetrate me. That's some pretty deep shit right there.

When you're focused on a goal or a dream, sometimes the only person who will understand it is yourself, and that's okay. Its okay to have no support. Those are the times you realize you only need one supporter. Yourself. Set some goals and deadlines, work in silence, premiere your vision, then clap for yourself. Celebrate yourself.

It used to really bother me seeing so many of my friends and followers under these celebrities' pictures with the heart eyes emojis but didn't bother to even acknowledge me? Why in the world would they easily praise a person who they most likely will never meet or get acknowledged by but a person they actually know and communicate with, gets nothing?

Big dreams don't resonate with small minded people, and that's okay. Your glow will intimidate many people. Shine anyway. These are the same type of people who will have your name in so much "they say" but not one prayer. Are we really worried about what people like this think? We shouldn't.

Do you. Chase your dreams. Be a free spirit. Live the life people are scared to live. Live so free in a way that when you're 80, you can say actually say, "I did everything in life I wanted to do". I believe that is life's greatest gift, to have lived the life you wanted, unapologetically. Forget all the reasons something won't work and believe in one reason it will.

May 1st, 2014

"He would've been 11 today. I still can't believe 11 years have gone by. Wow does time fly. I picture him in my head all the time. His first steps, his first day of school, and even his first heartbreak. I don't think anything in life prepares you for the loss of a child."

When people ask me how many kids I have, I have to think about it for a second. If I tell them four, they will eventually ask me where's my fourth as only three are around. I do have four kids though. I honestly hate leaving my son out because he is indeed my child but to shield the pain of talking about it, I usually just say three.

When I was nine months pregnant, I went to the doctor for a routine checkup. I was getting an ultrasound to make sure the baby was positioned correctly because my due date was approaching. I will never forget the look on the technicians' face when she saw the screen. Her eyes got big, and she started moving the transducer rapidly on my stomach. I asked what was wrong. She looked at me and said, "the baby has no heartbeat". She ran out of the room to get the doctor. I'm not sure if I didn't process what she was saying then or if it just hadn't hit me yet, but I kind of just sat there.

The doctor explained to me that because I was so far along, I still had to deliver the baby as a normal delivery. I had to actually go into labor and push the baby out. (crying)

I was given a special type of medicine to induce my labor. Shortly after I began feeling contractions. I was in labor for 6 hours. Six hours of pain knowing I was going to birth a child I could not take home. Part of me could not believe this was happening. I thought for some reason they had it all wrong. That maybe if I prayed hard enough God would allow me to deliver a baby that was indeed alive. Maybe my faith wasn't strong enough or maybe it was just a part of God's plan to take my son, but either way, I birthed a dead child.

He was purple when he came out. They could not tell how long he had been dead inside of me. He had a smell I would never forget. I can't describe it, but once you've smelled it, you'll never forget it. Death. I wanted to open his eyes so bad to see them, but I was scared. I held him for hours. Crying and crying. I couldn't stop crying. What had I done wrong? I hadn't done anything wrong. God's plans were just greater than my own.

We get into the thought process of wanting what we want, but never think about what HE wants. If we all take a moment to attempt to understand HIS will and way, then we could understand. I am a firm believer in everything happens for a reason. My child was taken away before he took his first breath for a reason. I have prayed on this pain for years. What I discovered was the reason was more so because of me than my child.

Through my suffering, I was taught empathy, compassion, humility but most of all, I was taught to trust God.

Purpose always outweighs your plans. God blessed me with an amazing platform, but before he could give it to me, he had to make sure I was in a position to heal the broken. So many of our "why me's" are translated into "why not you". God has prepared each of us to deal with tragedy, suffering, and pain so that we can help the next person, impact their lives, and change such a troubled world. We all have a story to tell about pain. Some of us choose not to share the story out of embarrassment, pain, or whatever other reason, but each of us has scars.

My challenge to you is to use your scars to help the woman next to you, the woman beside you, or the woman behind you. Let your scars tell a story of how life TRIED to break you but FAILED. Your pain has not been without purpose. There is meaning in it all.

I still deal with the grief and loss of my son around his birthday. I probably always will, but I have peace knowing that he has escaped the pain of this world and is happy in the arms of God. For that, I am thankful. I am also thankful God chose me to impact other women who have perhaps lost a child. Restoring hope is a beautiful thing.

June 9th, 2014

"Father's Day is this week. I don't even care. I'm not sure what would ever make a parent not love their child wholeheartedly. God, it hurts. I think sometimes it would be better off if I never knew him at all. I think the feelings of abandonment have left me seeking love from men that were never meant for me. Out of all the pain, I'm still trying to convince myself it's for a reason. Hurt by your own father though is something I don't think any child is equipped to deal with.

Still, I long for the connection between him and I. Still I wish he would just ask me to go to lunch or dinner. The love I feel for my children would never allow me to turn my back on them. How can he even sleep not knowing if his own flesh and blood is okay? All I can do at this point is let go and let God. Let God be my true father, refuge, and protector. Help heal me and give me the strength to forgive."

If you've read "I had to WomanUp", you know I haven't talked to my father in years. My father and I had a beautiful relationship up until he got remarried. His wife hated me because of the color of my skin. She was only 10 years older than me too so maybe that had a lot to do with it. I was 10 when he met her. She was 18.

My father is a weak man. Perhaps the weakest man I've ever met. I didn't realize this until I became an adult. I never understood how someone could walk away from their own child. Not because I had done anything wrong but because he decided to start a new life. I can't properly word the feeling but it's close to what death feels like. Like a piece of me died when my father walked away.

That feeling has affected me my whole life. I have constantly felt the need to hold onto dead situations and men that are toxic out of fear of losing and being alone. I have given men more of me than I ever gave my own self. That's a scary thing to even realize.

Most times in families, even when the father isn't there, we have brothers, uncles or cousins to look up to. I didn't. My brothers were train wrecks. One in a gang and one in and out of jail. Growing up, I watched both of my brothers beat on my mom. I can remember one afternoon my brother choking my mom so hard I thought her eyes were going to pop out of her head. My cousins were the same too. Deadbeats. My uncles were spread out on drugs and one, in particular, was a child molester. No looking up to anything over there.

I opened this book by saying that I was failed by the men in my life before I even got a chance to start my own life. Abuse, abandonment, and failure was accepted. I thought this was normal. It's so important to realize how bad of a cycle this is. We may not realize it, but we become programmed to believe this behavior is okay, and it affects so many areas of our life that we don't even realize. It's important to break that cycle. If not for us, for our children. To keep them from seeing what we've seen.

I haven't talked to my father in years. My brothers and I have shaky relationships and I haven't spoken to any of my cousins or uncles in years. I don't know where any of them even are. It used to bother me, but it doesn't at all now. Sometimes family can hurt you the most. In my case, family not only hurt me, family almost ruined my life. The men in our lives are supposed to our leaders, our providers, our protectors. In no way should we EVER accept anything less than that. If you've never experienced a positive connection with a male, please understand there ARE good men out there. Please do not think otherwise or settle for a half-assed one because that's what you saw growing up.

June 9th, 2014

(Part Two)

"Thinking about my own father has made me think about my children's father. He's seen the kids three times in five years. I don't know what to do. How am I supposed to explain to them their dad isn't there not because he lives in another state or is dead, but he's simply not around because he doesn't care. God this is not what I had planned.

I HATE him. I want to go flat his tires, spit on him, mace him. I just want him to FEEL what I feel. I just wanted to have my own family and be happy. I not only failed myself. I failed my children."

I met my kid's father when I was 16. He was 24. I remember lying about my age. I told him I was 19. At the time, I was a runaway. My mother was so strict. I wanted a taste of freedom. I got more than a taste of freedom. I ended up with two babies from a bum. The babies I would never regret. It's him I do.

I was crossing the street with my friend Tisha, I remember she said, "that guy is calling you". I don't remember the words he said, but whatever it was had to be kind of catchy because I got in the car. He was everything. Smart, funny, and caring. I had nowhere to go. I was sleeping on my friend's sofa around this time. He would rent hotels every night for me, buy me food, make sure I was okay, and of course have sex with me. I got pregnant. I was elated. I thought this was my chance at a new life. Mom, dad, baby. What a fucking joke.

I ended up going back to my mother's house around this time. I knew nothing about being pregnant, and I essentially needed the support from my mother. I just knew he would be around. Man was I wrong. He left. Cold turkey. I didn't hear from him my entire pregnancy. I pushed out Jadyn with my mom, and sister in the room.

Tracking him down was hard. He was nowhere to be found. While I could not find him, child support did. When he got served with child support papers, he made it his business to contact me. For two months he came around. Told me how he wanted to be there for me and the baby, how he was going to do better. The only thing he did was get me pregnant again with my son and got me to drop the child support case. I felt like a real idiot.

Over the course of the next few years, he was in and out. He would call at 2 am and I would answer ecstatic welcoming him to come over. I thought that one day he would have an epiphany and want to be with me and his kids. He never did. He was never active in the kid's life. He never cared if they had clothes, food, or shelter. He had abandoned his own kids the same way my father once abandoned me.

For years I fought through so many feelings about him. Hate, hope, and betrayal. How could I be so stupid to put not only myself in this situation but my kids? It has taking years to get over that hurt. I was so focused that my children would lack that I didn't realize as long as I'm doing what I need to do as a mother, they would not lack at all.

Being a single mother has made me strong. It has turned me into the woman I am today. Unshakeable with the outlook that ANYTHING is possible. It is… Single motherhood is not a death sentence. It's more so a journey of learning how strong you are.

My children today are teenagers. We have pretty much grown up together. We have unbreakable bonds. Sometimes in life, we have to view the positives instead of the negatives. Yes, he's not there, but no they never need anything. Yes, it has hurt me, but no it has not broken me. Yes, I wanted revenge, BUT God gave me something better. He gave me strength.

There is a bible verse I treasure. "I will repay you for the years the locusts have eaten". That promise to me is that no matter what bad happens in life, God will come through with better. Greater. More. I share that promise with you. For the hurt, the pain, the abandonment, and betrayal, God is going to give you something amazing. Don't seek revenge. Seek peace. Trust in his word.

Oct 30th, 2014

"Tomorrow is a big club night for me. I'm hoping to make some money! I haven't made any real money in months. I'm not sure why God is allowing Satan to attack my business. Maybe it's something he's trying to show me? Maybe it's time I exit out of the nightclub world. Maybe it's time for true growth and the nightlife industry isn't for me anymore."

I am a firm believer in God. I understand his power and promises, but I also understand his timing. I originally moved to Tampa, FL to attend school. I had hopes of pursuing my master's degree, and the colleges in the city I lived in did not offer those courses. Upon moving, I resigned from my job. I had plans to find a new job, but to be honest I was just more focused on school. I had a little money saved up, so I would be comfortable for a while anyway. I must've miscalculated some kind of way because the money I thought would last me for a while, ran out quickly.

I remember searching for jobs at this time with no luck. A promoter contacted me during this time on social media about hosting a club night. I agreed. The event ended up going so well, he asked me to return every third Saturday. I agreed. My night eventually got so big, I transitioned into doing every week. I was thrilled. Not only was I able to take care of my kids, but I was able to have a relaxed "job".

My new success and income lasted about 8 months. After that, things went downhill more and more until it completely died. What was happening to me? What did I do wrong? I had been faithful in my prayers. I had a heart of gold. I was obedient to the word. Why was what I took care of my kids with failing? Simply put, my season there was over, and God was getting ready to place me in another position.

When God is ready for us to "level up", he will give us signs it's time to transition to something new. If for some reason we don't take heed to those signs, he sends more signs, but these come in the form of actions. Things begin to happen to us that we cannot explain or even know the reason for. We start questioning why we're going through some of what we are, not realizing WE ARE THE REASON WE'RE STUCK IN A HOLE.

    I fought and fought to make my "promotional business" thrive. Nothing worked. I lost more and more money until I almost ran myself into bankruptcy. God sent me sign after sign to "move on" but I ignored. Hitting close to rock bottom is what shook me up and made me realize I needed change. Sometimes we get stuck on a chapter in our life and try to hold on to it so long that we don't even realize it's time to move on. This chapter may feel good, but I promise if you just trust God enough to move on, the next one will feel even better.

    God placed me in the nightlife industry to give me the skills I have today. I can negotiate contracts with talent and venues, I know what market prices for certain events are, and I know what to demand and expect with planning. All of these things have helped me develop my current business to what it is today. Once I was done learning those lessons, it was time to go to the next level.

I will extend that same knowledge to you. Know that life is broken down in chapters. You take a little from each one then move on with that wisdom to the next chapter. Never stay on one too long. No matter how good it feels, constantly be looking to "level up". Never end the quest for self-improvement, life-improvement, or even business improvement. Take what was given to you and prepare yourself for what's next on the list.

Nov. 2nd, 2014

"When I think about it, I don't have many "friends" anymore. I don't know if it's me that's the problem. Maybe I'm not a good person. I have tried to hold on to the ones I have, but nothing works. No matter how much love or support I give, I get none back. They only love me when they need something from me. They only want to hang out when it's something they want to do. I talk about my dreams, hopes, and plans but they never talk about theirs. Maybe I make them uncomfortable."

I had an interview not too long ago where I talked about the importance of losing friends. Yes, you read that correctly, the importance of losing friends. I'm not sure where and when we were taught that we had to go through life with the same people we met from years ago, but that thought process is wrong.

You will indeed meet some people in life that become your lifetime friends. Those, however, are few. The majority of people you meet are seasonal. They are meant to be around for a short time only. They enter your life and are there for reasons. They'll teach you some of life's greatest lessons, then their purpose after that is simply to leave. This is the part where most of us go wrong. We try to hold on to friendships with these people who are in reality just seasonal associates and not lifetime friends.

When I think about this time in my life, I was still surrounded by people from my early adult years. People who had nothing going on at all for themselves. I thought that me distancing myself or not being around them meant that I was a sell-out. We were alike in so many ways because we came from the same place, but we were nothing alike at all.

I had gone to college, none of them did. I was trying to build a business, none of them had one. I wanted to lay a foundation for my children, none of them understood what that meant. I am by no means saying I thought I was better than them, but what I am saying is our outlook on life was completely different. What we wanted out of life and where we were going was nowhere in the same direction. You don't always have to be on the exact chapter as someone else, but you at least have to be in the same book.

My "dreams" were causing my "seasonal" friends to view me differently. They thought that I was acting different and distancing myself when in reality, I was on my grind and trying to build something for myself. That's a warning sign on its own. When "friends" can't see or support your vision. Those are not friends at all. Personal growth is learning when to leave the seasonal people behind. Leaving them doesn't mean you don't love them, it means you value your growth, and of course, you can still love them! Just as we shed dead skin cells so that fresh new skin can emerge, we also have to shed dead connections so that fresh healthy connections can be made.

I'm going to use an analogy of a fish in a pond. Did you know that most fish grow according to the body of water they're kept in? Imagine having shark potential but being kept in a goldfish bowl. You would never grow in the way you were supposed to. You have to jump out that small pond where you're surrounded by tadpoles and go jump into an ocean with whales.

Once you go jump into the ocean with whales (other like-minded people), it's like a breath of fresh air. You'll start being motivated and pushed in ways you've never thought possible. You will start to make positive connections with people who actually want to see you do good, and that's what friendship is all about! A lifetime support system with someone you're bonded with in so many different ways.

Jan. 26th, 2015

"I met an absolute AMAZING man last night. This might be the one! I've read in so many books that you know instantly when you've found "the one". He's the one! Don't know anything about him except his name, but all the other stuff we'll figure out later. All I know is the attraction def is real and unlike anything I've felt before"

I met McKinnsley one night at a social event. As soon as he walked through the door it was like instantly we looked at each other. Soon as eye contact was made, it was over. He asked me questions no man I ever just met has asked me before. He asked about my purpose in life, my passion in Christ, and about my goals. It was so refreshing to have someone ask questions regarding things of substance instead of just regular topics. Needless to say, we left together that night. No, we didn't have a passion filled night of sex, but what he gave me was better than sex. He gave me intimacy.

After that night, we were inseparable. We went to charity functions together, we went on trips together, and we even participated in each other's children's activities together. I was convinced this was THE ONE. He was smart, funny, handsome, God-fearing and great, great, great in the bedroom. Even though we had only been dating about 6 months at this time, I was patiently waiting for my ring. It never came. I can't point the blame at him as to why he and I didn't work. As a woman, I will take responsibility that my broken-ness play a huge part.

For years, I had been essentially involved with scum bags. Men who were grown boys and lacked the respect a woman deserved. I had been so programmed to dealing with these types of guys that when I finally got a "real man", I didn't know how to treat him. I accused him of cheating if he was gone too long, I made claims women were calling if his phone rang at night, I would get upset about small things and have major blowups, but above all things, I didn't give him the respect he deserved as a man. My insecurity, my past, and my failure to WomanUp led to me losing one of the best men I've ever had.

That part hurts… Bad.

When he started pushing me away, I didn't even realize it. I can see now that's what he was trying to do in hopes maybe things would get better, but at that time, I viewed it as he didn't want me in his life anymore. The more he wanted space, the more I didn't allow it until I essentially ran him away. God sent me what I had been praying for, but my actions ran him away. That's something I will forever have to deal with. During this time, I became pretty depressed. I was also kind of embarrassed about what I was going through, so I chose not to talk to anyone about it.

An old childhood friend of mine, Marley, out of the blue called me around this time. It was so refreshing to speak to an old friend who actually knew and loved me. I told her about some of the problems McKinnsley and I were having. She said something that sticks with me still to this day. She said, "God will either bring him back to you or give you a new one who will be willing to stick around". A man who loves me enough to realize I'm broken but stays anyway. I had so many questions. Does love like that even exist anymore? Do I deserve it?

    My answer is yes. Love like that DOES exist. Love like that is real. The stuff we see in the movies DOES happen. We ALL have a shot at love no matter how broken we are but in order to get that caliber of love, we have to become the kind of woman who deserves that type of love. We can point fingers all day at a man for not sticking around or loving us properly but are we truly deserving of that mans love? Do our actions make him want to never leave or do they make him want to never return? It starts with YOU.

You have to fix yourself and love yourself before you can love him. A man who loves you will help piece you back together, and a man who loves you will help you unpack your baggage but any man who has the slightest amount of respect for himself will never stick around in a situation where he is accused, abused, neglected and talked down on. Don't lose your soulmate over your own insecurities.

.

May 16th, 2015

"We had our very first WomanUp last week. That event has changed my life. I cried the whole time. When I went to speak, I broke down. Bad. When I left, however, it was like I left as a new person. I felt more complete than I ever have. People actually waited until after the program to speak to me.

They thanked me for being so transparent. We cried together and even prayed together. The feeling of doing something purposeful is unreal. I don't know where God is going to take me with this brand, but I have faith it's going to be something magical."

I dedicate this chapter to chasing your dreams. I don't have a life lesson for this chapter. I instead, will only offer encouragement to never let whatever it is you want to do in life die. It's no better feeling than to see something you dreamed of come to life. I had planned a women's empowerment event for years, but either lack of funds or just flat out fear kept me from doing it, but man oh man when I finally did, I knew right then everything that had happened to me in life had led me to that very moment. The moment I turned my struggles into strength.

It takes a lot of courage to chase your dreams. Some people live their whole life and never pursue anything they have wanted to do. Either lack of resources, money, lifestyle changes, marriage, or the birth of children causes them to let what's inside of them go. That's one of the worst mistakes in life we can ever make. I can't possibly think of being 60, 70, or 80 with a whole bunch of "I should haves".

This event to me was truly a game changer. What we lacked in the number of attendees, we made up for in how many lives we touched. I stepped out on faith and even though it didn't come together as I wanted it to, it served its purpose. One of my favorite sayings is "whatever is done with purpose, will always prosper". It may not immediately, but if we stick to it, it ALWAYS will.

There will be some discouraging times, but in those moments it's important to focus. Baby steps. A little progress is better than none. Reevaluate and adjust if necessary, but don't ever stop chasing what God has put in your heart. It doesn't matter how big your dreams are, they are possible. You don't need to be perfect, you don't need to be the best, you don't need to be an expert. You simply need to have the courage to live the life you want.

Sept. 4th, 2015

"This day is bittersweet. I think of the life my mother lived, the goodness she sowed, and the love she gave. I also think of how she was taken away from me so early. The smiles, the tears, and the friendship, I can never forget. If no one in this world has ever truly loved me, I know she did. Happy Birthday, Mom. One day I'm going to make you truly proud."

Losing a parent is something that we all must face. I think we don't focus on it often because we feel like we have a lifetime to share with them. I remember my mother always saying, "You're going to miss me when I'm gone". I would tell her she was talking crazy, and that I was going to have her forever. I lost my mother when I was 25. She was only 55 years old.

I had gotten a call from my sister that my mother had been admitted to the hospital for chest pain. I didn't think anything too major of it at first because I knew my mother was a fighter. When I saw her though, it's like I knew she wasn't going to make it. She had to have open heart surgery for a blocked artery, but the doctor said she was young and healthy and would be fine. The surgery lasted over 24 hours. She made it out successfully but coded shortly after. I will never forget the feeling I had being told my mother was dead.

Why her, and not me? Why take someone who chose goodness in life? Why take someone who meant so much to so many? These are questions I still cannot answer. The next few weeks were so hard for me. Picking out gravestones, writing her obituary, cleaning out her house, and even finding an outfit to bury her in was gut-wrenching. I think I was able to hold it together though because I wanted to make sure above all things, I buried her like a queen.

During this time, I was silently suffering internally battling with feelings of loss, regret, sorrow, and heartbreak. I can't tell you what got me to the point where I decided I didn't want to be here anymore, but the decision had been made. I was going to kill myself. I had convinced myself this world was full of pain, and there was no reason to live. I had been praying so heavy during this time for peace, and guidance. Nothing was happening though.

On the eve that I had planned my suicide, I was in bed wide awake and alert reading my bible. I had been crying and asking God to show me some kind of sign all day. The next part you may be skeptical about, but I swear to you this is no fictionalized story.

My mother walked into my room. She had on all white and was glowing so bright that I could not fully see her. She sat on my bed. We started talking about all types of things, and the reasons it was important for me to live. The conversation was so real that I asked her, "Why would you have us pay all this money for this funeral if you're really not dead", she got up, smiled and replied, "Oh I'm gone, but I'll always be with you". She then started to walk away.

I tried to run after her, but my body would not let me move. I tried to scream, but no words came out. When I couldn't see her in my sight anymore my body released. I ran into the living room screaming, looking for her. The guy I was dating at the time asked me what was wrong. I shouted, "My mom was just here, where is my mother!", but she was gone. He tried calming me down, but I wouldn't. I cried that whole night.

When people ask me why my faith is so strong, I reference this story. I have always believed in God, but this gave me the ultimate reassurance there is something beyond this world that cannot be explained. God knew my faith was running out, and that I was indeed at my lowest. He gave me something in the midst of my darkest hour. He gave me not only hope but a reason to live.

It's important to know no pain in this world is greater than your purpose. No amount of pain is ever worth taking your life. It's one of the most selfish acts we can ever perform. The same way I was motherless, my children would have been. When I didn't see it that way, God sent me a sign to force me to. I'm not sure what your pain has been or may ever be, but what I will say is, God will give us everything we need if we're silent enough to hear him, still enough to feel him, and patient enough to trust him. You can call it whatever you want, but GOD IS REAL. Trust in him, even when you can't trust in yourself.

Dec. 25th, 2015

*Life isn't all good, but it's not all bad either. This year has been one of my best years yet. This was my year of detoxification, spiritual peace, and letting go of everything in life that has hurt me. For the roller coaster ride, Lord I thank you! The ups and downs have prepared me to enter into my best season yet. 2016 is going to be my year of consecutive wins. I speak it, I believe it, I claim it, IT'S **MINE**.''*

I wrote this entry on Christmas day. I remember being so excited. I think I was even more excited then the kids were because I was able to get them everything on their Christmas lists. My son had given me a card he made. Inside of it, he thanked me for being a good mother and giving them everything they needed. It was and still is the most beautiful gift I've ever received.

Reading the card made me think a lot about my own life. If I was able to give my children everything they needed so easily, then why couldn't I give myself what I needed too? I was tired of letting my past define me. I was tired of allowing others who did so little for me to have such a strong impact on my life. I was tired of crying. I was determined at this point to make 2016 my BEST year.

The trials and tribulations that had haunted me for years were released. The "you can't do it's" were wiped away from my memory. The "no's" were rejected. The negative opinions were declined and returned to the senders along with a prayer for them. The pain was turned into POWER. Can you guess what happened next?

The doubters became believers.

God prepared a table for me to eat while those who hurt me watched. (Thou preparest a table before me in the presence of mine enemies. My cup OVERFLOWETH.) My blessings truly overflowed. Even if I had a weak moment or a setback, it was like God was already working on something else. Everything was working out in MY favor.

The people who rejected me for years, God allowed them to have a front row seat to MY show. The Aicha show. The show that never disappoints. The show that never has a rainy day. The show where I never stop smiling. The show of everlasting happiness.

The place of peace I'm in today is simply because I was tired of not living. I was tired of pretending to be happy. I was tired of not allowing God's promises to work in my life. Before I could get to this point of peace, I had to make the hardest decision I've ever had to make. I had to kill me. The old me had to die so I could be resurrected as new. It sounds easy but to let go of everything inside of you and to build yourself anew is hard. It's pretty painful too. Allowing yourself to face reality, forgive, and let go are three of the toughest challenges we will ever face.

Life is a lot like boxing. You have to protect yourself at all times but not so much that you don't have a chance to feel. Feel everything. Feel the hurt so that you appreciate happiness. Feel the fear so that you appreciate the calm. Feel the anger so you appreciate the joy. Feel the pain so you appreciate the pleasure. Feel the disappointment so you can appreciate the enjoyment. Feel rejection so you can appreciate acceptance. Feel the times everything goes wrong so that you appreciate when everything goes right. Feel the loss so that you appreciate the win.

God doesn't promise to never allow pain. What he does promise though is he will never give us anything we're not strong enough to deal with or allow anything that is not done for purpose. I truly thank God for my darkest hours because I know how to appreciate these bright days. I am a continued work in progress. I'm nowhere near where I want to be but by the grace of God, I'm nowhere near where I used to be either. I pray that if you've ever experienced anything that I shared in this book, that you are freed. What you release, can never hurt you again. Please remember that. Always.

I have enclosed extra pages in this book for you to write your thoughts and to reflect on anything that you may have related to in the book. Remember what you free yourself from can no longer hurt you.

I have also reserved this area for you to figure out what your purpose is. To do this, as I explained in the book, write down everything that means something to you. Anything you may be passionate about. When you get to the one that makes you want to cry, you have then found your purpose.

Made in the USA
Middletown, DE
15 September 2019